# The Arc
## *of*
# Grieving

## POEMS FOR
## THE JOURNEY

## SUZANNE WEISS MORGEN

*For Diana,*
*may this book be a caring and compassionate*
*companion for you and those you serve*
*who are grieving.*

*my thanks,*
*Suzanne*

**WHITE MORNING PUBLISHING**

**LOS ANGELES**

# The Arc of Grieving: Poems for the Journey

**Author:** Suzanne Weiss Morgen

**Illustrator:** Marjorie Sarnat

**Book Designer:** Marty Safir, Double M Graphics

### Publisher

White Morning Publishing
Los Angeles, California

For inquiries please visit:
www.whitemorningpublishing.com

**ISBN-13:** 978-0-578-74980-8

*In memory of my loving parents*
*Hank and Goldine Weiss*
*I miss you*

— SWM

# Preface

My mother died in late January, followed by my father in early August. Losing them both so close together was a life-altering, overwhelming experience. I was devastated, bereft, bombarded, orphaned, and struggling to cope and carry on. I found myself desperately searching for some way to process my profound hurt, heartache, and pain and to understand what had happened to me.

My saving grace came from the poetry that poured out of me. It helped me to express the kaleidoscope of feelings coursing through me—to untangle complex and unfamiliar emotions. For me, this writing became more necessity than choice. It was often difficult to keep up as my thoughts raced wildly. The poems provided an opportunity to find some order in the chaos: appreciate, reflect, consider, remember, release, forgive, rage, weep, and finally heal.

This collection of poems began as my personal journey of grieving and mourning my parents. However, it became much more as I expanded my thinking and explored what happens when a loved one dies. These poems are not only for me. I wanted them to encompass the feelings and experiences of anyone faced with a death. I spoke with numerous others who have been through the loss of a loved one, and I expanded my writing to include their experiences as well. I wanted to write about grief's complexity in as many forms as possible so that everyone who is affected by the death of someone they loved can find relevance and connection to the words. Bereavement is, of course, a fundamental human experience.

Death knows no boundaries. Losing someone can be a traumatic experience requiring loving compassion, introspection, empathy, grit, and true resilience. These poems are meant for you, your family, your friends and loved ones. They are for any support group, religious community, or person who has been touched by the grieving experience. Read them silently or aloud, alone or in the company of others at a service, memorial, or other gathering. And feel free to read them in any order that feels right.

May these poetic words provide an outlet, a vessel, and a voice for your own complicated thoughts and feelings, and may you find comfort, solace, recognition, and healing peace. You are understood, and you are not alone.

Suzanne Weiss Morgen

# Acknowledgments

I am so grateful for every embrace and comforting visage I encountered during my time of grieving. Receiving the openhearted love and support of family and friends was invaluable and deeply appreciated.

Writing this poetry book was a solitary endeavor. However, I must thank the wonderful village of people who provided me with their generous and insightful feedback during this heartfelt project. They all helped in various ways to bring this collection to fruition. I am listing them here in alphabetical order:

Sonja Chandler, Baruch and Claire Cohon, Susan Diskin, Miriam Elkins, Susan Harris, Rosanne Keynan, Adam Kligfeld, Susan Laemmle, Carol Mason, Karen Peterson, Bob Safir, and Lynne Sullivan.

I want to especially thank Christine d'Arc Taylor for her vital editorial insight and guidance. Additional thanks to Marty Safir and Marjorie Sarnat for their collaborative energies bringing skilled artistic sensibilities to my writing.

I am particularly thankful to my husband, Henry Morgen, for his enormous support and patience.

# Contents

## 3 Reemergence 37

# 1
## It Begins

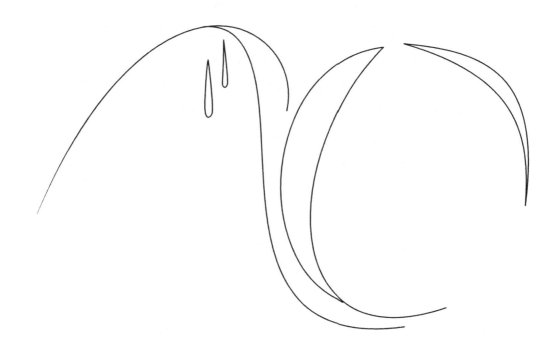

## IT BEGINS

It begins when someone you love dies

A multitude of emotions are unleashed

Running wild like rowdy children let loose

Colliding and riding the crest of a mighty wave

Don't expect them to behave

Not right now

As they crash and smash into one another

Anger and blame

Guilt and shame

Sadness, heartbreak, pain, and remorse

Of course, there are no simple answers

Sometimes there's even a crazy mixed-up kind of glee

Your suffering loved one is finally free

It begins with a cacophony, too

Dissonant and demanding

Commanding inner voices rail and rage

People and papers you're forced to engage

Everything suddenly so out of place

Buried regrets you just can't erase

Proceed with caution, care, and heart

For when it begins it's a difficult start

And do what you can to stay real and true

That's really all anyone can ask of you

## LAST REFLECTIONS (FOR HER)

I stood by her bed

Head to head

So close

So intimate

Trying to be strong and still singing her favorite song

And then the hospice nurse suddenly said

She's gone

It had been so long

And now she was gone

There were 16 breaths a minute

Then 14, 12, and at the end 2 or 3

Hard to see

The last breath came

No pain or agitation for her

But choking and gasping for me

She was free

And I was momentarily lost in tears and shock

11:37AM on the clock

All the years and memories flooded back

I didn't have a large stack of IOU's

Just I love you's

And gratitude

Go

Be

Let the pain cease

Now is your time to rest in peace

## LAST REFLECTIONS (FOR HIM)

I stood by his bed

Head to head

So close

So intimate

Trying to be strong

All along

And then the hospice nurse suddenly said

He's gone

It felt like a knife

When just weeks before

He was so full of life

Hard to see

The last breath came

No pain or agitation for him

But choking and gasping for me

He was free

And I was lost in tears and shock

4:00PM on the clock

All the years and memories flooded back

A gigantic stack

Like a sudden storm

Raging and running

So many, so fast

Present, past, and now the last

I didn't have a list of IOU's

Just I love you's

And gratitude

Go

Be

Let the pain cease

Now is your time to rest in peace

# THERE IS A MOMENT

There is a moment when everything changes

The earth opens and anything you've ever known rearranges

Your heart goes to pieces

Your normal life ceases

You find yourself clinging and slipping and tripping

And into the creases and depths of your being you fall

You try to recall all the good times

Before, long before

Times with sweet, simple memories all of us store

The wonderful moments of sharing and caring

Oh that was daring, and how are you faring?

Now what lies ahead is uncertain, uneven, unruly, unkempt

And no one is exempt from the loss of a loved one

How do you go on?

Family and friends, like water and food

Can help to sustain you, maintain you and soothe you

Lean on them, and let them prop you up and pull you along

Without pushing

Just comforting, cushioning

Through the minutes and hours and days

In ways you can only imagine

Until time and loving memories mend and heal you

Repair your rips and fears and tears

And weave your torn tapestry back together again

# WE NEED TO MOURN

Tattered

Torn

Shattered

The sharp edges cutting into our hearts

Ripped apart by death

Take a breath

We need to mourn

Let the ride begin

A rollercoaster of emotions

Dense, then sparse

Gentle, then harsh

Quiet, aching

Then shouting and suddenly shaking

We need to mourn

We are born

We live, we laugh, we cry

And the years fly by

They soar and sweep and arc

They ebb and flow

And when they go

It all ends and death comes

There is no more to do

Not for you

But for us

We need to mourn

And say goodbye

And say goodbye

## I WILL REMEMBER

I wasn't ready to let you go
I wasn't ready to miss you so
Over the days and years
Well past the early grief and tears
I will remember
I will remember
You

I wasn't ready to say goodbye
I wasn't ready to let you fly
Still I must let you go
Believing you certainly must know
I will remember
I will remember
You

And when I think of you I see your face
The love you gave, time can't erase
You will be missed
Your memory treasured
Feelings of emptiness cannot be measured

I wasn't ready to face the end
I wasn't ready to comprehend
How much I needed you
You were among a precious few
I will remember
I will remember
You

# FIRST YOU GRIEVE

First you grieve

And then you mourn

And then you get hold of a very large horn

And let it blast and cry out

To express the outrage and pain you feel at this terrible loss

And then you cry and sob

And somehow try to do your job

Although you really don't want to do anything

Except maybe attempt to remember the beautiful, special, happy times

The times when all was good

And all was well

Before the hell set in and death came

Play the memory game

Remember the sweet togetherness

And all the little things that made a full life

Good life—long life

Remember them

And it will gradually get easier

And the tears will become trickles instead of waterfalls

And all that will remain is the joyful memory

Now and forever

## CHANGES

I was so unprepared for the changes

I knew, of course, that illness would change you

Take off weight

Bleach out your color and vitality

Force your mood to a darker place

A starker, sharper space

But it's not just you

I'm equally, perhaps even more, unprepared for the changes in me

The unrelenting stress, sadness, and unrest

The accelerated march into unknown territories

Tributaries overflowing their banks

Tanks and armies doing battle

Your moans and groans rattle me

Piercing my increasingly raw psyche

I'm taken for a loop and sent 'round the bend

Again and again out of control

Lunging and lurching

There's no rehearsing here

It's only too real

Fears, tears, and all

Calls in the night

And evolving plans of action that may or may not be right

If I could just step back and observe

It would be clear that these changes would occur

Look at what I must traverse

A slow-moving hearse

Life and death

Your last breath

These are vast and lasting changes

Wish for them or not

That's what I've got

## TEARS

Tears are heavy and messy and wet

And yet what better way to feel the pain

Let the sniffling and sobbing become your refrain

Your loved one is gone

And you remain

Today, tomorrow

Through hurt and sorrow

Tears jump over fences

And break down defenses

They run like a river of truth

Sometimes they trickle

Sometimes they swell

It's hard to know, predict, or tell

And some days will simply be hell

Just let the tears flow

And go where they must

Follow your heart

Let go and trust

No GPS can show you the way

Take it hour by hour

Day by day

And though tears may hover

Just know you'll recover

Surrender

Be tender

And always remember

## IN DEEP WATER

You're thrown in the deep end when someone close to you dies

Submerged, weighted down, and gasping for air

There's been a huge tear in the fabric of your being

You struggle to regain some modicum of control

How do you stay whole?

You feel hyperactive and almost comatose at the same time

Deluged by memories

In this unfamiliar ocean where everything seems wrong

Thankfully, you're strong enough to keep your head above water

Even as deep in as you are

Keeping the bar of expectations low helps

As you flail your way through the hours and days

You'll probably have to swim in the deep end for a while

Pull up every bit of information that can help you survive

You are, after all, the one still alive

And you must carry on

Use songs and stories

A connection to God and the universe

Anything that helps pull you through

Just do what you can do

And when the sinking pain comes

Don't succumb to the deep water

Carry on to honor the one now gone

## THE NEW REALITY

Shocked and sad

Rocked to the depths by your death

Clinging to faith when fairness and reason feel lost

I am accosted by a new reality and forced into acceptance

Thrashing about, my mind wanders in a vast desert of burning sand

Stranded and unable to discern any direction

Then suddenly my thoughts shift

I am desperately attempting to escape a raging storm

An angry sea determined to swallow me whole

My soul cries out to you, my love

Can you hear it when I sing your praises?

I call out

But I can no longer fall into your warm embrace when despair contorts my face

Sobs rob me of even my ability to speak

My soul scarred

I regard myself as an injured survivor

You were the source of so much of my inspiration

Somehow able to make the trials and troubles of life seem bearable

Even fixable

We could work it out

No matter what it was about

I must now navigate without you to lean on

Strengthen my own backbone

Dare myself to exist in this new world

This new reality deep within me

Your life lessons are stored

You were adored

And now I will devote myself to carrying your legacy forward

Accomplishing all I can

Comforted by your abundant and sheltering love

## A DIFFERENT KIND OF LOVE LETTER

I never felt the length of the day

Until I had to face the night without you

How cruel this separation feels

It wields its might like a samurai sword

And like the fractured board of the karate master

I am broken apart

I should have seen it coming

Things were not exactly humming

But the drumbeat of death came to a fortissimo so abruptly

It shattered my steadfast denial

For a while you were so steady

And we were so ready to resume our normal existence

At your insistence, I kept my worrying to a low bar

You were the shining star of my life

I never felt the warmth of the sun as I did on our last walks together

No matter what the actual weather

I felt only the radiance of you near me

Wherever you are

I believe you can still hear me

And so I will not shout or cry out

I'll only whisper in the gentle loving way I know you treasured

I love you in a way that cannot be measured

## NUMB

I feel a bit numb

I know you died

But I haven't cried

I feel a bit dead inside

Somehow my limbs still function

My eyes still see

And my ears hear the kind words of consolation

My mind is busy buzzing with memories

Furious and fast

Sorting through the past

Your death was not a total shock

We had taken stock and knew you were fading away

Day by day growing more weak and weary

Hanging in that twilight place

No real trace of the person I once knew

Not really you

Not anymore

Death's door open and ready

Your steady march relentless and determined

I have laid you to rest

I have done my best

And although the tears won't flow

I want you to know

I love you

## PEOPLE ARE KIND

People are kind

They come to offer you cookies and casseroles

Comfort and consolation

And stories old and new

More than a few of which you've never heard

Some are absurd; some are delightful

And some are more than a little insightful

You are grateful they have come to pay tribute

And kindly distribute their heartfelt condolences

Yes, people are kind

As you unwind the lifetime of your dear one lost

It's important to reminisce

Both for you and for them

It's like giving a final loving hug and kiss goodbye

Words can be as beautiful as the moonlit sky

And though remembering may make you cry

Don't hold back

No point in that

No saving face

Embrace the moment

Just surrender and let people be there for you

Their care and compassion can soften the blow

Roll with the kindness

Give thanks and be glad

For amid the sadness

You'll find that people are kind

# 2
# In the Midst

## THE PROCESS

I am both master and slave to a painful process I knew nothing
about before you died

Grieving is leaving everything that feels normal behind

I have been in control when necessary

But just as often I have been beaten down into low, dark places

Spaces usually open and available

Seem closed to my mournful pleas and wails

Flailing

Bereft

Nothing left

So vulnerable and volatile

I have read volumes about the pain, the loss, the transformation

The length and depth of the grieving experience

It doesn't matter

It's only real now that you have gone

So long to every summer, autumn, winter, and spring we would
have spent together

You have been sent on a new journey

And every season will now give me reason to remember

A birthday, an anniversary, a holiday, a song or a dance

Always a chance to smile at a memory

When I have the strength, that is

And the length of time seems right

As I work this process through

Day by day

Saying goodbye to you

## FEELING

Feeling too much

Feeling too little

I'm in one corner and then the other

And everywhere in between

Screaming, crying, and just silently trying

Every which way to get through the day

I sometimes wish I could hire a surrogate

Someone to carry the load for months and months

Endure the nausea and fatigue

But no such luck

It's mine to own

Solely, completely

Honing my skills as a survivor

Moment by hour by day

Managing the tolls I have to pay

Feeling whatever I'm feeling

For whatever time I must

I can only trust

I am still alive

And I will survive

## SOMEHOW

My world shattered

And somehow everything that mattered was instantly rearranged

To say things changed when you died would be crazy

Things exploded, imploded, and reloaded

My rearranged world could no longer include you

You were gone

And I had to dig to the depths and back to stay strong

I had to learn now who I was

That's what losing someone does

To me and you and anyone who has lost someone dear

We're still here

The emptiness takes time to fill

Be still

Wait for the memories to glow and gleam

And stream into your mind and heart

The perfect aura reminiscence can allow

And just know it will happen

Someway

Somehow

## IT'S TEMPTING TO SIMPLY SAY

It's tempting to simply say I'm relieved

It's been so hard to see you in pain

The constant refrain of sobs and screams

Careening on the rollercoaster of your last days

And then at the end

The free fall into the silence palliative medicine and drugs can bring

Let the angels sing

And welcome you to the relief, to the release, and to the peace

But pardon me as I clarify

As I began, it would be tempting to simply say I'm relieved

But I'm also enraged and wounded

Sad in a way I didn't know even existed

And probably would have insisted I could not sink to feel such lows

But the blows are all too real

It's more overwhelming than I could have imagined

Right now, I only want to imagine you in a better place

On your new journey of spirit

Death has come

And you have gone

But I will cherish all you were

For as long as I live

Knowing you are at peace

That is the comfort I give myself now

## STRETCHED

Your death has stretched me to where I am reshaped and reconfigured

I don't think I could have reconstructed myself in this way

Only a momentous play by the hand of death could make this change

My very being feels strange

Empty without you

I somehow doubt you are truly gone

Surely it's just an especially long sojourn

Have no fear

You'll reappear

Because if you really have left my life forever

I must accept the unacceptable

Your loss is final

Going forward for me will also mean going backward

I expect I'll run circles around memories of you

Curving and swerving from here to there

Squaring off against the demons of death

Catching my breath and fighting on

Attempting to be strong

There will be no forgetting you

That's for sure

Only figuring out how to endure

## AFTER

After you died I cried forever

At least it felt like it would never end

It was outrageous

And probably contagious within myself

No shelf space left for anything else

Taking big risks and descending rapidly

I just hoped the hard landing wouldn't destroy me too

You left in such a ruthless way

Never a chance that you could stay

On a day I will never forget

A day I will always regret

When will I recover?

God only knows

My mantra now is "purposeful patience"

We'll see how it goes

As my shaky structure grows stronger

All I know is that you are no longer

I must dig carefully to shovel away the hurt and dirt

Brutal work as I follow my brambly, unpredictable pathway

Every day

Until there is some end

## KNOWING

How could I have known?

Knowing means you have some idea of what's really going on

That feeling is gone

I've grown increasingly suspicious

As twists and turns thrust themselves into my fractured world

My footing becomes precarious

I am hurled down a rabbit hole by your death

I try to pull together precious strands of my former life

Threading the needle now takes immense patience, persistence, and faith

There must eventually be a settlement

 Some negotiated peace when the turmoil will cease

And some level of normalcy will return

Knowing what I now know has robbed me of tranquility

Death is a thief

No abilities I currently possess can arrest the feelings of unease

More and more I know less and less

I can only urge myself to doggedly continue on

Even though you are gone

And I hardly know where I belong

I must believe that in the end there will be some light

Some right

And some good from all the hard-earned knowing yet to come

## EXPECTATION

I expected to recover more quickly than I did

But once the lid came off

And my turmoil boiled over

It was a completely different timeline

You just can't predict how quickly or how long

Grieving is a melancholy song

Everyone has to set their own tempo

And navigating the shifting dynamics can make you go a little mad

It's like the worst headache you've ever had

Some people whisper

Some people wail up and down the scale

Truth is

Recovery comes when you're good and ready

Don't get too heady

Just keep walking

And talking it out if you need to

If you think it will help you

Don't prod or punish yourself

And above all else

Expect the unexpected

# EVERYWHERE I LOOK

I'm going through your things

That's what death brings

And everywhere I look

Your life plays out before my eyes

Another closet, another surprise

Sometimes I feel like a spy

Prying into your papers and pictures of days gone by

Wondering why and how and when and where

Just so much there

I'm staring and caring too much

Pieces of you and pieces of me

Far-flung memories

Tangled together in boxes and piles and files

Everywhere I look

I'm faced with decisions

What to keep, what to sell

What to tell

Lingering, pondering, protecting

Propelled into another time

Transported back through the never-ending stacks

That's what happens when you die

I'm trying to concentrate, calculate, catalogue

All of the clothing, furniture, jewelry

What a bewildering, tiring task

I'm exhausted, enlightened, exhilarated, exasperated

Cleaning out your home I'm stepping back

Into medical records and musical records

Albums of artists long gone

And rooms filled with books

I should certainly look

At all those photos you took

Some are of people I don't even know

Family and friends from long, long ago

I will try to ask others still alive and able

We'll sit around the table

Attempt to make sense of those folders and drawers

Filled up so deep and dense

Everywhere I look

There are things to determine, remember, consider

And I'm not a quitter

I can't know for certain just what you would wish

There's a dish and a plaque

Awards and cards

It's so hard as I whittle

Little by little

I've found things I'd given you tenderly tucked away

Touched that you saved them to cherish another day

I can now surely see I've answered the call

Given my all to this tour of your life

And everywhere I look

I know it's the end

I must comprehend it's complete

And live with my memories

Heartfelt and sweet

## THAT'S GRIEVING

Never walking a straight line

That's grieving

Weaving and wondering when you'll break down

And where you'll rise with tears in your eyes

Up and out of the crash site

No right or wrong

No short or long

Only the sweet song of treasured memories

Familiar tunes now in a foreign key

You can't see ahead

And when you look back

It only reminds you of your enormous loss

Toss your expectations out

And use whatever is about

To reach, pivot, and connect

To anything and anyone beyond little you

Who knows what's true

Everything can be a clue

Just know that no easy path will get you out of these woods

There's no route of perfection

No designated direction

You'll have to navigate on your own

Potholes, puddles, and all

Stand tall

And be proud of who you are

Acknowledge the dear ones gone

They helped shape you all along

And stay strong

You're doing your best

Only healing time can do the rest

That's grieving

## SOMETIMES I REALLY NEED TO FEEL MY SORROW

Sometimes I really need to feel my sorrow

Deeply and completely

I weep and write

And it seems all right

At least for a while

And that's what matters

I look back on my heart in tatters

And I realize the deep hurt is gone

Not that I don't long for your loving smile

Or the style and grace you brought to every situation

God knows, I keep attempting to cultivate your good qualities in me

We'll see

Any changes I make will be a success

It's forever a work in progress

Sometimes I really need to feel my sorrow

It makes it easier to face tomorrow after tomorrow

Being true to the memory of you

# LIVING IN THE GREAT UNKNOWN

Living in the great unknown

With you gone

I feel both weaker and stronger than ever before

Confusing feelings hard to ignore

Refusing to allow me a settled sense

Spoiling my sleep

And confounding my waking hours

I am not the person I was before

Not any more

Living in the great unknown

It's burden that can't be measured purely by weight

Although the weight is great

It goes beyond just the heaviness

Cascading into a bewildering haze

A moment-by-moment maze of conflicting emotions

All whirling and swirling at top speed

Like a crazy baton twirler

Leading some wayward parade

Living in the great unknown

Makes me feel alone and crowded at the same time

Off balance

Like a bad rhyme or a rhythm that can't keep a steady beat

There's a crushing heat

And yet I still have the chills

I wonder sometimes when I'll emerge

When I'll be able to purge myself of the angst and despair

And care about normal everyday life

I can't hurry my journey through these uncharted waters

If I push, there is a pull back

If I climb over, I end up underneath

Thunder and lightning couldn't create more dramatic conditions

So many decisions and provisions to be juggled

I have huddled

And then harnessed my energy to find a way out

To learn more about the great unknown

It treats everybody differently

But most significantly

All I really can do is just be patient

And stay true to the new me

Living in the great unknown

## YOU WERE NOT PERFECT

No one is perfect

And you certainly were not

There were times when we fought

And our words got caught and fractured

It could be rough when we disagreed

My heart would bleed a bit

And I'd have to sit and simmer down

But through it all

I knew you loved me

You loved me more than you could ever really express

As if somehow saying it aloud too often caused you distress

Yet you showed up for me

Stood up for me in so many ways

There were displays of valor with sweet victories won

Done to perfection

Because you truly did care

And you were there

You could be stubborn and demanding

Reprimanding and withdrawn

But then a new dawn would break

And you would awaken with the warmth of a thousand suns

"You are my treasured one," you would say

And your display of love and kindness was true

You were complex and smart

Your puzzle parts not made for amateurs or the faint of heart

Sometimes so sure

And other times wary and scared

You cared beyond what most could fathom

And fortune smiled on those who knew you

Yes—you were not the perfect one

But when all is said and done
You could surprise beyond compare
You were always there for me
Until you had to go

## THE ARC OF GRIEF

Grief is personal, perplexing, profound

Ebbing and flowing

Exposing itself to every emotion imaginable

Fashioning a full spectrum of colors and textures

All mixed up with the bitter taste of loss and the salty flavor of tears

Grief steers you around like an errant, erratic teenager

Running you ragged in all directions

There is the pulling in

The pushing on

The difficult balancing act of ups and downs

And then finally a kind of letting go

Slowly the denseness and darkness begin to lift

And you're given the gift of breathing into a more open and available space

Your stiff ribs soften

Your knotted gut releases

And pieces of your mind and body begin to reintegrate

Wait

Don't hurry

Be kind and gentle as you enter into this fragile new territory

Reconciliation, restoration, recovery

Is there a certain inevitability to it all?

The fall, the rise

The hit-between-the-eyes surprise

The coming to grips with so much that's new

That's what grieving can do to you

# 3
# Reemergence

## MY GRIEVING JOURNEY

When I began my grieving journey

I had plenty of fuel

Because any fool knew it could be a long road

With no clear path and no real map

Anything was possible

Detours and ditches were not out of the question

And did I mention the fires and floods?

Catastrophe brought to my door?

Particularly the disaster of your being no more

I have careened and collapsed along the journey

Running on fumes when fuel ran low

I cursed you for going

All the while knowing it was inevitable

You had to leave

And I had to grieve

Many steps of this grieving journey have been incomprehensible and unfathomable

But it's the only way to get to the other side

What a ride

Everyone's journey is so different

But not indifferent

Everyone who loses someone they love must embark

Start with your broken heart

When I began my grieving journey I had no idea when or where it would end

Eventually the slog became easier

I'm not certain it's exactly over

But I don't feel the same unrelenting pressure anymore

Not like before

Your formidable goodness illuminates my memories

And my thoughts of you have become more buoyant

I can hope and dream again

And when I bring you to my mind's eye

I no longer instantly cry

Instead I smile

And I thank you

You helped make me who I was before

And who I am now

I'm not sure how

But it happened along my grieving journey

# US WITHOUT YOU

You died

And left us wounded survivors

Reeling in a tsunami of emotions

An earthquake in our lives

That opened cracks and crevices

Some tiny

Some immense

Intensity overtaking serenity

Who knows how long the cycle of mourning and grieving will last

We just know that whatever has been

Is no more

Those we adored in life

We now hold in heartfelt perpetuity

We mark your place

And let you rest

Moving ahead

Doing our best

Our only plan

To honor you

Through all we do

## A LONG ROAD BACK

It's been a long road back

Trying to get on track

Detours and ditches

Innumerable hitches and accidents along the way

It's been a long road back

Trying to get on track

A marathon run with a gun to my head

Threatening me

And forcing me to keep on moving

Keep on proving

Lessons learned both mundane and profound

And no allowance for slowing down

I proved to myself I could do it

Bit by bit

Wit by wit

Clawing my way back to normalcy

Whatever that may now be

It's been a long road back

Trying to get on track

My heart has bled

So much has been said

I have weathered the bleakest, blackest of times

Finally the finish line is in sight

And even if everything isn't perfectly right

It was all worth the fight

Taking the long road back

Trying to get on track

## THIS YEAR

This year we've been to hell and back

Sustaining heavy casualties along the way

What can we say?

Loved ones lost

The cost has been great

The weight immense

The heartbreak intense

We are healing

Though definitely still feeling their absence

And we are different

Realigned now

In mind and heart

New start

Over, under, and through it all

Falling and rising and wising up

New and old and bold

Time has moved on

And we, the living, have moved along too

Hoping we are making them proud

And carrying our backpacks filled with memories

## RESOLVING TO HEAL

You died

And I was left to heal the wounds

It was too soon

We needed more time to apologize and recognize the good in one another

Time to retune the dissonant chords in our relationship before this final farewell

Your death felt like the opening of a gaping sinkhole

Ready to swallow me whole

Death takes a huge toll on even the most honest and healthy relationship

But a flawed and troubled past makes you feel like you're sinking way too fast

I created a ladder to help me climb out

Every scrap of positivity alleviating my doubt

I know that carrying extra baggage can be heavy

And I am determined to continue my life's journey with a lighter load

And on a better road

So wherever you now are

Near or far

Rest in peace knowing that my healing has begun

And will continue until it's done

## THE GRIEF IS LIFTING

I'm beginning to feel the sun again

Does that mean the grief is lifting?

Sifting through old photos sometimes makes me laugh

Does that mean the grief is lifting?

I know there will still be moments

Times I'll be surprised and overtaken by raw emotion

But it's happening less

And I'm smiling more

I feel like I'm coming ashore after a long storm at sea

Free to revel in the warmth of your beloved memory

You will always be the light to me

A shining star wherever you are

But now

I can finally live more fully in my own life again

And I can more clearly comprehend

How much you gave the world while you were here

I can appreciate you with good cheer

And I am thankful

Today, tomorrow, and always

And that must mean the grief is lifting

## SOMETHING DIFFERENT

You are here and there

And everywhere our minds and memories allow us the pleasure of your company

In the ground

And in the clouds

Found in the tiniest moments

And tucked into the pulsating chambers of the healing heart

Beating on and on

Gone only in body

Your spirit spinning and soaring

Exploring a universe of new promises and possibilities

You touched us and trained us

Your death has rearranged us

For without you we've become something different

Redefined

Reinvented

Presented with innumerable opportunities to learn and grow

Lost and then found in another land

We are learning with time to understand

Please know how much we love you

As we mark your place

Remembering you with gratitude and grace

# I DON'T KNOW

I don't know exactly where you went

Or where you are

But somehow I can sense you haven't gone far

A comforting whisper of a gentle breeze

The way a stranger can put me at ease

I will miss your earthly form

So warm and welcoming

But I wish your spirit release and freedom

Freedom from illness and pain

Nothing left to explain

Soaring with great abandon

Light and unencumbered

Ecstatic

Emphatically not burdened as you were here

No fear

I shall mourn you vigorously and passionately

It is my right and my privilege

I don't know exactly how it will go

I'll just follow the flow of my tears

Be it days, months, or years

Every moment something special and unique

Just like you

## THE OTHER SIDE

There is no magic moment when the buzzer rings

The stings just hurt less over time

Your heart is released from purgatory

And slowly your story morphs

It dwarfs and extinguishes the chaos of those early days of grief

With relief, progression, and some form of closure

A new direction appears in your expanded universe

Your life demands reflection

And when you see yourself more clearly under the bright light

To your credit, you do not run

By choosing to stay and work through the messy process of healing

Congratulations are due

You move into the open arms of life's renewed embrace

Traces of grief and sadness may still play upon your heartstrings

After all, someone you loved died

Yet without knowing exactly how or when

You've made it to the other side

## HOPE

I had lost my grip on hope

But now I feel it firmly taking me by the hand

From the desolate land of despair

I've emerged to greet the promised land of the public square

With people and activities everywhere

And I am ready and interested in interaction and conversation

Reservation and isolation have departed

Replaced by a blossoming reunion with the outside world

I feel unfurled and eager to fly

Like a buoyant flag soaring in a wide-open sky

You will remain with me

Present and eternal

Your kernels of goodness and wisdom in permanent storage within

But now the next stage of my life is meant to begin

I feel newly choreographed

With movements to take me far beyond the boundaries of my grief

You are deeply rooted in me

Like a flower too beautiful to ignore

Rest assured

You will be showered with love forever more

## EMERGING

The butterfly emerges from its cocoon

And so I too break free

Shedding my slumber and stupor

Entering some new longitude, latitude, attitude

Reworked

Optimistic

Non-specific, but with a pulse of life returned

Blood pumping

Meridians tingling with energy

My organs all at work doing their jobs

Especially my beleaguered heart

Its brokenness slowly repaired by time and prayer

I stare now at this welcome hopefulness

More awake, attuned, freshly groomed and ready

I can walk and talk and discover something new

After you there is still a life

My reassembled life with your essence safely cradled

Like some cherished piece of heaven with me here on earth

Rebirth after death

New depth and breadth

And for all this

I must say

Thank you

## YOU WERE

You were funny and sunny and sharp as a tack

No one would dispute that

Smart and steady and always ready

You were generous

Not only with money

But with the honeyed warmth of human kindness

Your blindness to others' foibles and faults was a wonderful quality

You were a friend to many

An amazing ambassador for good

Always doing all you could

You had a quiet way of putting others at ease

Not just to please

But to help make things whole

I can honestly say

You were great

And that's not just the latest news bulletin

It's been true all along

And now with you gone

I will miss your gigantic heart

Your love was a gift

Right from the start

I will hold tight to my memories of you

For you were one of the righteous few

## COMING TO A PLACE OF PEACE

Coming to a place of peace and acceptance

That was the goal

To become whole again

In whatever manifestation or assemblage that might be

Claiming back the pieces of me

Coming to a place of peace and grace

I dreamed and hoped it would materialize

Realized by my palpable struggle

Peace is so much more appreciated after the hard-fought battle

And there has been plenty to rattle my calm along the grieving path

The point being

Freeing myself to finally celebrate your memory with delight

Lets me know I'm going to be all right

Coming to a place of peace

And sweet release

# IN THE STILL SWEET SILENCE

In the still sweet silence of the morning

Your face appears in my mind's eye

To say goodbye?

To say hello?

I don't really know

But I am so happy to see you

Your countenance looks healthy and strong

And an otherwise perfectly ordinary day is transformed

I see you free of pain

Of pressure and distress

Looking your best and in your prime

Beaming with magnificent light

It all seems right

I also hear your voice of reassurance

My celestial insurance policy

You sport no angel's wings

Nor do you sing any heavenly serenades

But the point is made

You will remain a part of my life

A different relationship for sure

But at least available in some pure and private way for consulting

Resulting, for me, in the blessing of a newfound connection

You will always be a welcome spirit in my life

And I will be forever grateful for any still sweet silences you choose to fill

# In Your Own Words

*Personal pages for your thoughts and feelings*

Made in the USA
Columbia, SC
29 March 2021